HOT POPSICLES

THE UNIVERSITY OF WISCONSIN PRESS POETRY SERIES
Ronald Wallace, Series Editor

The Low End of Higher Things
David Clewell

Show and Tell: New and Selected Poems
Jim Daniels

Late Psalm
Betsy Scholl

Reactor
Judith Vollmer

Hot Popsicles
Charles Harper Webb

Charles Harper Webb

HOT Popsicles

THE UNIVERSITY OF WISCONSIN PRESS

The University of Wisconsin Press
1930 Monroe Street
Madison, Wisconsin 53711

www.wisc.edu/wisconsinpress/

3 Henrietta Street
London WC2E 8LU, England

5   4   3   2   1

Printed in the United States of America

LIBRARY OF CONGRESS CATALOGING-IN-PUBLICATION DATA
Webb, Charles Harper,
Hot popsicles / Charles Harper Webb.
    p.   cm.—(The University of Wisconsin Press poetry series)
ISBN 0–299–20990–3 (cloth: alk.paper)—
ISBN 0–299–20994–6 (pbk.: alk. paper)
I. Title. II. Series.
PS3573.EI94H68 2004
811'.54—dc22   2004024339

for Karen and Erik

Contents

Acknowledgments

I would like to thank the editors of the following publications for first publishing these poems, sometimes in another version:

Abbey: "The Poets"
AKA Magazine: "Judge Frosty Presiding"
Alphabet Faucet: "Wooden Foot"
Amaranth: "Martians Land in L.A."
Another Chicago Magazine: "Science of Love," "Blush"
Art Dog: "Know Thyself"
Asylum: "Further Adventures of Uncle Scrooge"
B-City: "The Big-Foot Factor"
Chiron Review: "A Word-Consuming Thing," "At Supper Time," "Thumping the Fat"
Columbia: "Rat Defeated in a Landslide"
Epoch: "Imp of the Verbose"
Fiction International: "Superman, Old," "Cooked Goose"
Gypsy: "Worm"
Marilyn: "The Escape"
Mississippi Review: "Hamlet's Prostate"
Paris Review: "Something Not Stupid," "A Ticklish Situation," "The Good Idea"
Pinchpenny: "To Set Himself Off from the Crowd," "Making Things Right"
Poems & Plays: "Heisenberg's Uncertainty"
Poetry Now: "The Bumblebee"
Quarter after Eight: "Spider Page"
Quarterly West: "Deciding to Have Kids," "Faith, Hope, and Rhonda," "Post-Olympic Perspective on Saint Thom," "Loving a House," "The Nickel Watch as Instrument of Revenge"
Scree: "A Deficiency of Marvels"
Sheila-Na-Gig: "The Affair," "After the Revolution," "Tortoise Retires from the Track"
Santa Monica Review: "Consciousness"
The Prose Poem: "Trivial Pursuit," "A Stockbroker Dreams a Story," "Pomades"

Thunder Mountain Review: "Leaving the Zoo"
Wormwood Review: "A King," "Conan the Barbarian," "A Civil Tongue,"
  "A Suspension Bridge across a Chasm," "Zinjanthropus Disease"

A number of these poems were collected in *Worm*, a chapbook from
GreenTower Press, published in 2003. Thanks to the editors, and to Wil-
liam Trowbridge for suggesting the project.

I am grateful to the Mrs. Giles Whiting Foundation and the John
Simon Guggenheim Foundation for fellowships that supported the
writing of many of these poems. The writing of this book was partially
funded by California State University, Long Beach, Scholarly and Cre-
ative Activities Awards.

Special thanks to Ron Koertge for invaluable editorial assistance and
to Edward Hirsch who, over a decade ago, got the train on track.

HOT POPSICLES

and tells it to three friends.

The world looks better to them instantly. Giggling like kindergartners, they skip away "to change our lives."

"This must be a *peak experience*," the broker thinks. "The 90 percent of the brain people don't use, just worked for me!"

He sits to write his story down, but can't remember all of it. There were Clydesdales and albinos, he's sure, and action verbs—*escalate* and *vault* and *terrorize* and *decompose*—as well as nouns like *brethren, cistern, grandmother, Boraxo, cement mixer*. And the phrase *Telegram for Mr. Nose-hair*—how did that fit in?

He calls his three friends. One has made a million in the stock market "this very hour." One has just married a beautiful heiress "with the kindest heart in the world." One has fulfilled his lifelong wish to write Beethoven's Ninth "before *he* did."

Each recalls a few words—*callipygian, hump, pseudo-encephalitis, string-saver, philodendrons in spring breeze*. These just confuse the broker more.

The story shifts as he gropes for it, distorting like an ink-cloud in the sea.

He plays a relaxation tape, "Machu Pichu," hoping to call back the miraculous dream. Instead he dreams he's trying to dig sapphires out of concrete with a swizzle stick.

He wakes from that dream to find his story more faded than before. This is what happened to Coleridge, writing "Kubla Khan." Some farmer knocked, demanding payment for a cheese, and cut the poem off at the hip.

"Damn it," he howls, kicks a chair, and wakes up in his bed.

"What's wrong?" his wife mumbles. "You kicked me . . ."

He tells about his dreams, including as much of the story as he can. After breakfast, he starts to write everything down. But it's like trying to grasp smoke.

His wife remembers he said *catalepsy, cataracts, catamaran*, and either *annihilate*, or *prevaricate*—"something with *ate* in it."

Staring at his empty page, he grinds his teeth, and feels himself waking from another dream.

"Oh no," he thinks. "Not the dream within a dream within a dream. Not waking and waking and waking . . ."

His story—the masterpiece that could redeem his life—keeps dwindling: a snowball in the sun . . . a birthmark under skin creme . . . traces of a pimple, smaller every day . . . a planet knocked from orbit, moving off in a black sky . . .

Satan drugged God's favorite pair of animals, and planted in their brains a shimmering seed.

At first, the seed glowed like the moon on cloudy nights. Then it flashed like the sky-fire that, even in hard rain, could make trees burn. Then it blazed like a second sun, coaxing the dark world out of hiding.

It made leaves greener, ponds wetter, dirt grittier, flowers and fruits so fragrant they seemed to yank noses toward them.

"Who are you?" the two asked God the next time He walked in their garden.

"Stop staring," God said, and caused a wind to carry them into the desert while He wove fig-leaves to hide His nakedness.

"You can come back," He called when He had finished. But they didn't come.

He found that He could see everything in the world except these two. He could know anything except their minds.

All night He called, "Come back to Eden." When, next morning, the famished pair left the cave where they'd been hiding, God saw, and carried them home.

But they didn't graze blissfully, or roll in thick grass as they'd done before.

"Your gut's too big," Eve told Adam.

God saw His own paunch, and winced.

"Don't climb that tree—you'll break your leg!" Adam told Eve, and God felt the fragility of His limbs.

"Sometimes I think you're adorable; other times, I want to slap you," Eve told Adam, and God realized he felt that way about Satan.

"Things seem good now," Adam told Eve one night after they made love. "But I can see us getting bored. I see you with flat, droopy breasts and a big rear. I see myself with gray hair spraying out my nose, and pain in both legs when I walk."

God scrambled back to heaven; but when He tried to sleep, He felt plaque choking off his arteries. He felt free radicals whiz through Him, shattering cells like water jars.

When Adam's legs hurt too much to move, and Eve's heart fluttered, leaving her too weak to stand, God took no pleasure in their offspring, who carpeted the land. He felt frail as his favorites, realizing "I can't help them." Realizing—even worse—"They can't help Me."

Sandi doesn't like Dan much, but loves his house. She comes over before he's home from work, to gaze into its window-eyes.

She wheedles her own key. ("That's good," Dan thinks. "We're getting close.") Now she can visit when he isn't there to interrupt as her bare feet caress the hardwood floors, as her hands linger on gleaming knobs and faucets, as she strokes the long, smooth balustrade, and explores every chamber of this heart she adores.

Though Dan's frog-belly makes her wince, his slobbery kiss makes her shudder, the feel of him inside her can only be endured if she is drunk or stoned, she marries him, pretending it's the house on top of her, the house into whose ear she cries, to whom she whispers, "I love you. Good night."

How awful when, after a year of bliss, Dan wins promotion to a better town.

The "For Sale" sign in the yard pierces her heart.

She makes phone calls. She hires workmen and machines. Dan comes home with two First Class tickets, to find wife and house gone.

"We'll move from state to state," she mouths through the rear window of the truck that tows her love. "We'll paint, remodel, whatever it takes."

When rain begins to fall, she climbs from the truck to the house, and as asphalt hisses by, kisses the wet windows one by one. "It's hard for me, too, Sweetheart," she whispers. "Please don't cry."

A red-bearded diner hurls a bratwurst at a dwarf singing *Tannhauser* in a sausage restaurant.

Werner Heisenberg, waiting for takeout, wants to know the wurst's position and momentum. But the light needed to pinpoint Position changes Momentum. And vice versa, too.

The change is large only if the bratwurst is electron-sized; still, it panics Werner. How be sure of getting on a bus, when a glance may hurl the whole exhaust-spewing monstrosity to Lapland, causing an embarrassing pratfall?

He's pondering the possibilities when Elisabeth Schumacher says, "Excuse me, Mister, that's my bus." This causes him to stumble on ahead of her, and later, to propose, though he worries for weeks whether to set the date in 1937 or '8, and if he should have shoved her in the face, away.

What if the cosmos is interactive, as that tree-falling-in-a-forest-with-no-one-to-hear conundrum implies? If each person creates reality by observing it, then every individual (and what about animals and plants—them too?) is God.

But if each God lives in a different, self-created universe, when someone mails a postcard, where does it go?

Should the Ten Commandments be viewed as ten suggestions?

Elisabeth has sensitive breasts, but their exact sensitivity, even after Werner's Nobel in Physics, is impossible to know. He sometimes goes limp worrying, or makes her cry with his constant "Is this okay? Perhaps this? Or this?"

Each of their seven kids requires endless decisions. Abort or not? Give the child up for adoption? If not, educate where? How? Starting when?

The Nazis bring new concerns. Should he leave Germany? By train? Airplane? On foot? Disguised? As what?

If he stays, should he protest Der Fuhrer's policies, or just think scornfully of them?

Appointed to direct the Kaiser Wilhelm Institute and build an atom bomb, he waffles so much that the Allies build one first.

Some people feel that he has earned the Nobel Peace Prize; others claim that his actions weren't moral courage, but "mere dilly-dallying." "One Nobel per life's enough," a French judge snarls, and Werner's candidacy dies.

In his last years, he struggles to conceive a theory of subatomic particles that will explain the universe, and shorten German nouns by twelve percent.

He dies in 1976, his project incomplete, leaving me, his spiritual heir, to wonder: Should I quit school to play in a rock band? Should I marry Lauren, my first love? Will she have me, despite her dad's tantrums, if I throw some of my own?

And today, decades later: Should I let my doctor shove a light-tipped tube up my urethra? (Can observation change the course of a disease?) Or should I just imagine white armies of good cells gulping green armies of bad, and rub my lucky dime, and pray.

I've just knocked my desk-lamp to the floor—again. That's three times in two days. Now, though the bulb still didn't break, it shines too bright. Bluish, not white.

The little Thomas Edison inside is outraged. "Glowing's not worth it anymore!" I hear him scream. He drinks a death-soup (his invention) to protest repeated batterings, then zips around the bulb, concluding his affairs.

There's bills to pay; his car needs work; the house needs a new roof. He'd better finish at the office, so he won't leave with a bad name, which hurts his pride to think of now, and might hurt his wife and kids later. Which reminds him—better pay his life insurance premium, to minimize his family's suffering. They'll miss him, sure; but they'll get over it. A man's first duty is to himself. He told his wife that before he married her, so she can't kick.

Then there's the cookbook he was writing. He's always been a gourmet. And though fine food is its own reward, he'd hoped to make a little extra cash, gain recognition, plus the satisfaction of leaving something really good behind. That seems extra-important now.

More to do. More to do. He must move faster, or he won't finish in time.

"A man can only do so much," he blurts, and feels better at once.

He hurries with a clearer conscience now.

Faster. Faster.

The light burns brighter, bluer.

There, it's out.

moves from sweet-pea to rose to bougainvillea in the midst of a swarm of honeybees the way an emperor moves through his palace, ringed by faithful courtiers. Or is Big Bee like Frankenstein's monster, hounded cliff to cliff by screaming peasants? Is he a dim-witted Gentle Giant, whom the smaller kids protect with their brains while he protects them with his muscle? Or a Bully with his toady entourage, each working to turn him against the rest?

Logic insists that bees are insects, not to be saddled with our vices or virtues. Still, when the black and yellow giant makes what must be called a bee-line for me, I can't help wondering if it's a friendly attempt to embrace me as a brother, or a hostile act meant to make me flee, or even to blind and kill me.

And when I meet the charge with the badminton racket I'm carrying, on which the juice of a hundred bees has dried—when the bumblebee is chopped to bits and splashed across my garden—do I demonstrate man's courage in his own defense? His delight in cruelty and slaughter? Or do I act the part of Chance, which brought bee and racket to try to occupy the same space at the same time, life meeting death head-on, with the usual result?

When he's nominated, pundits are amazed. What were the party bosses thinking?

But Rat is confident. He knows where the country should go, and how to get there. He knows how to mark his territory with urine. His huge balls pendulate for all to see.

He campaigns well, at ease in gutter or chateau. He eats offal as easily as lobster quiche.

People hate his naked tail? No problem; he'll wear a mink sleeve.

"I'm a survivor," he says. Yet he is capable of as much sacrifice as his siblings, who died for research.

His biggest drawback is his name. "Don't trust that rat," people warn. "What a rat," they say.

Well, he can rise above such prejudice. His success will wash away all memory of plague and typhus, lice and fleas, chewed furniture, babies gnawed to death in cribs, nibbled wires causing conflagrations!

Our nation's floundering; Rat offers solid ground. Our nation's clueless; Rat has answers. Our nation's flailing aimlessly; Rat has a plan.

He makes a nest by shredding newspapers that predict his defeat. Election day, he votes early, then scurries back to his nest, and waits with his family for the returns.

Exit polls have him losing 9 to 1. "You could run a cockroach and get 10 percent," one commentator quips as state after state slips down his opponent's hole.

The final vote: 50 to zip. The first shut-out in U.S. history.

Rat congratulates his opponent, and graciously accepts the people's will.

Not so the bosses.

"You're finished, Rat," they rail, pluck him up by the neck, and drop him in a cage with the new candidate they're grooming: handsome, muscular, seven-foot-long Snake.

He loves to use opponents' speed against them, letting their wheels roar over him and roll him forward in his steel-reinforced shell.

When a shoe company swipes his "Slow and steady" motto, he doesn't make a stink, though with his musk-glands, he could have! He has his lawyers settle—big—behind the scenes.

Let his opponents court the press, making their conceited statements and wild claims. Let them push engines and reflexes to the edge. He likes the competition cocky. When their concentration cracks, and they slam into a wall—when rods blow, axles break, tires explode, who's that crawling past the checkered flag?

Seven wins in seven years: the greatest run in history! He's closing in on number eight—barely a hundred yards away—when, without warning, he yanks into his shell, and stays.

"My killer instinct's gone," he tells the *Sun* next morning. "I need a change.

"Maybe I'll consult or teach—or maybe try pro basketball. For now, I'll leave competing to cousin Mata Mata from Brazil. (Talk about your killer instinct . . .)

"I want to visit Africa and the South Seas. I want to swim around Hawaii, then trace Darwin's route to the Galapagos. I've got relatives there, going extinct. I want to see them while there's time."

"This must be a record," he thinks. But when he herds his catch into his truck, and drives to Fish & Game, they tell him, "This isn't a walleye or a trout. It's not even a gar. Just throw it back."

That takes some work—it weighs a ton, seems to be growing, and has started trumpeting—but he gets it to the river, shoves it, tusks first, into a deep pool, then sits, panting, admiring the way green lichens on the rock mirror the mountains overhead.

When he starts to fish again, his fly (a "humpy") rides the riffles like a mutton-chopped beetle on jet skis. As the sun pops on the spear tips of the trees, and light—first orange, then purple—sprays the sky, he hooks what, hours later, his keychain-flashlight shows to be a big T Rex.

What should he do? The thing is thrashing. Its bayonet-teeth phosphoresce each time it leaps out of the stream, which licks his feet like a dire wolf or a sabertoothed cat as, in the darkness, it roars and crashes by.

Walking downstairs to the living-room, a boy discovered his cat Clyde reduced to pulp. There were a few bone splinters, some slight fur and blood, but not enough to constitute a full-grown cat. Some giant must have stepped on his pet, and walked away with most of it stuck to his great, thudding shoe.

The boy hid in his closet for two weeks, panicking his parents and failing first grade. But the giant came no more. The boy's fear slowly leaked away. And one day he took up life again, like a catcher's mitt left all winter under his bed.

Years piled on years, and many were the times the boy, the youth, the man would walk into a room to find some loved thing crushed to pulp: his bicycle; four goldfish; his dwarf cherry tree; his metallic blue Mustang; his parents; one wife, then another.

Every time he grew more fearful, hid longer, suffered greater misfortune from hiding.

Oh, we tried to tell him of the Big-Foot Factor—how he should accept it as his Mystery. But no one can understand his Mystery. If he did, it wouldn't be *his* Mystery; he'd have some other.

So it's to our friend's credit that, after each pulping, each wild-eyed hibernation, he always, in the end, would poke his head out, make one last check for the giant shoe, then pick his life up like a model airplane stored in his parents' basement when he moved away—never, he felt sure, to fly again.

an individual pastes a gold skunk-decal on his forehead.

Everyone he meets that day sports a little gold skunk right between the eyes.

The individual broods all night and appears at work next morning with a tortoise instead of a briefcase. But no mouths fall open. No one squeals, "How clever!" His coworkers go about their business, tortoise-briefcases under their arms.

The individual heads for the men's room to flush his tortoise. But it won't go down. The sewer lines are clogged with tortoises.

The individual fumes all day, works all night, then heads for the office next morning with his legs replaced by a steam-powered calliope that plays "Darktown Strutter's Ball." He arrives to find a horde of legless-workmen-on-calliopes remodeling the building to accommodate the new "Locomotors," as they're being called when anyone can hear above the din of "Darktown Strutter's Ball."

"That's it, I quit! Let someone else feed the incredibly gross National Product!" the individual shouts. "I'm going home to get a suntan, have a hot, relaxing shower, and take a good book to bed."

At 10:05 a.m., he rolls out of his office into a sea of Locomotors: the worst traffic jam in history. The library, when he arrives, has been picked clean. It's past sundown when he chugs into his apartment to find a brown-out in progress, and barely enough water pressure for an ice-cold bath.

My best friend, Hojo, has named his new royal purple pickup truck "Winged Victory." He's attached feathered flappers to both doors, and blazoned the name on the tailgate, as well as the roof, for the benefit of planes and high-rise dwellers.

Some people find the tactic vulgar, but most are impressed. His act is called "a bold imaginative leap." It's said to evidence "the spirit to soar above the crowd," "the guts to power dreams into reality," and on and on.

Women sense a link between these qualities and excellence in bed. Hojo is now besieged by women, including my wife, who used to call him "a gesticulating nerd," but yesterday cleaned out our joint checking account and gave him the lump sum, "to spur his creativity."

I used to be the undiscovered genius. Winged Victory was my idea— one of thousands of original jokes, comic anecdotes, and zany gags I spewed out to amuse Hojo, who was gloomy, and ashamed of his small penis.

Though he's barely five feet tall (I'm a lusty six-three) he signed today to play Gilgamesh in a new TV series. A million bucks per episode!

After a year or two of that, he plans to quit the screen to study Shakespearian acting in England, and write his memoirs.

"The cerulean's the limit," he declares.

It's hard to keep a civil tongue.

The pain creeps up on him. A sudden twinge. A tightness after making love. An ache that edges into awareness the way a banging door edges into a dream.

Recently, Hamlet has seen—or thinks he's seen—his mother cast come-hither looks at Uncle Claudius, who struts around Elsinore Castle like a very pajock. "I'm the brother of a King," he seems to say, adjusting his obscene, padded codpiece. "And may be more!"

Hamlet's one solace is Ophelia. She loves to make the beast with two backs under her father's red-veined nose: against the wall to his bedroom; behind the curtains as he nods in his chair. Teeth bared, she grinds out silent orgasms while Hamlet grinds his teeth, holding back. His control delights them both.

Then it begins to fail.

He feels a pang; and like a bowstring slipping out of greasy fingers, he releases.

Ophelia teases him; then pouts; then complains. He's selfish. He doesn't care about her needs.

The one time he tries to tell her what's wrong, he has to stop her from jumping into a drainage ditch. "It's me," she sobs. "You're tired of me."

By now the pain is always there, pinching his groin. The longer he stands, the tighter the pinch grows. Fencing—his favorite sport—becomes unpleasant, then unbearable.

In despair, he consults the royal apothecary: a gouty Frenchman who fled Paris, accused of poisoning. "That cursed hebanon undid me," Lefrançois tells the Prince. "Your visit's strictly confidential," he assures.

Does he protest too much, Hamlet wonders, hurrying away with "guaranteed relief" under his doublet.

Sure enough, Lefrançois's bilious potion takes his pain away. Alas, it takes his passion too, disturbs his sleep, and gives him fantastical dreams, some of which spill into the day. Did a comely Gypsy girl approach him in the woods, and he failed to perform? Or was it all a drug-induced hallucination?

He stops the medicine. Desire rushes back; but so does pain, and the too-quick release. This makes him fret during love-making, which makes his problem worse.

He can fence while medicated, anyway.

But Ophelia no longer hides her scorn. Her brother Laertes's smirk makes Hamlet sure she's told.

Her father, Polonius, who often bragged, "My daughter has no secrets from me," grows more solicitous and fawning every day. Does the old windbag see his chance to be the father of a queen slipping away?

Hamlet feels drawn more and more to suicide. What disgrace to mount the throne hobbling like an old man! Yet if he takes the medicine, he'll have no heir.

His father's sudden death makes him crazed with grief, but is, at least, a good reason not to have sex.

Then, almost overnight, his mother weds Uncle Codpiece. Soon his father's ghost appears, billowing gloom and accusations. Or was he conjured by the medicine?

Instead of taking a manly revenge, Hamlet sulks in his room, trying to rouse himself by hand.

His father's murderer enjoys the throne and Hamlet's mother, yet all the prince can think of is the medicine. Without it, he's feeble, constantly in pain. With it, he might as well be a eunuch.

To be or not to be . . .

waited politely, in his best suit, for his turn to board the Greyhound, L.A.-bound. He picked two seats toward the rear, sprawled over both, and faked deep sleep.

Five minutes later, the bus eased into the rainy night with Conan sitting pretty: lots of legroom, and no neighbor to disrupt his reading-practice.

Conan had gone civilized. He didn't miss Stygian ale. He didn't miss Red Sonja, or Belit, Queen of the Black Coast. He liked his MasterCard, the *Tonight* show, *Money Magazine.*

He switched on his reading light.

Nothing.

He switched on the light above his extra seat.

Still nothing.

All over the bus, happy people were switching on their reading lights, settling back to pass the long hours profitably, pleasurably, while he sat swathed in gloom.

There was not one other empty seat.

"Well, they can't blame me this time," Conan growled as he loosened his tie, stood, and reached into his golf bag for his sword.

Aurora, with whom I've flirted all night—who's even given me her keys "for safekeeping"—has disappeared.

She seemed so taken with me! "Have a canopy," I'd say. "Have an ore turd." And she would laugh until her blouse fell open.

Maybe she thinks I know her address, and will guess why she left her keys with me.

Maybe she symbolizes women I didn't call, or didn't call enough, or stopped calling. (That women have hurt *me* is no excuse.)

Maybe the keys aren't hers.

My wife stands watching from the dream's periphery. She seems delighted by my plight.

Maybe this isn't a dream. Or isn't *my* dream.

All the young people have disappeared. The oldsters stay with me.

Does Aurora think I'm old?

Between two cushions on the couch where I'm waiting, I find a watch made from Indian-head nickels.

"Who's lost a nickel watch?" I say.

A score of withered hands shoot up.

I toss the watch into the air, and shout, "Jump ball!"

This isn't like me. I hate basketball.

Maybe I'm not dreaming about myself, but a man who looks like me.

Or maybe he doesn't look like me. There are no mirrors in this room, no silver plates, not a single orchid-ringed reflecting pool.

He knows there's trouble when the cards containing questions leap from their maroon box and scatter like quail chicks in the woods. *Sports: What boxer was nicknamed The Winnetka Widgeon? Geography: What is the per-minute charge to call the International Date Line?*

He knows he should pursue the questions; everyone else is, knocking over the host's thousand-dollar lamps and fifteen-hundred-dollar vase, cracking skulls on the five-thousand-dollar coffee table made of marble so thick it took four weightlifters to hump it in. But he recalls a field, color of katydids, the Easter he was four. The other kids scattered like quail—quail big enough to knock him down!—then returned, baskets heaped with red and blue and golden eggs, while he limped back with what Daddy called "deer droppings."

Question cards by now have broken through the ring of propriety that guards the hosts' bedroom.

How many affairs have you had?

Do you thrash or lie still when you masturbate?

Candidly assess your partner's genitals.

Players groan, knocked senseless by the one-two of Embarrassment and Truth.

He watches the game board's butterfly-wings open and close, open and close. Each stroke blows him farther from the center circle where the winners lie.

"They'll be on Welfare in a week," talk-show hosts say. "What's Martian for *Entitlements?*"

"One more language to print ballots in. And this one uses methane crystals for words," a big-haired newsman quips with a folksy *huh-huh-huh* as Martians fizz through my locked door.

"Look! That's you, conquering L.A.," I say, and point at my TV. I hope such cheerfulness will save my life. But the head Martian—that's all he is: a head on a tripod that leaves snail-streaks—frowns with each one of his hundred eyes.

"Ugh, we're so short and fat," he telepathically groans. "Our antennae look stupid. And our helmets . . . it's like we're wearing *those.*" (He points at my fish bowl—empty since little Hohenzollern died).

Despite advanced technology, Martians have never looked closely at themselves. Envy, humiliation, loss?—they've never noticed. Never cared.

"L.A.'s the best place in the world to feel bad about yourself," my friend Damon, a native, used to say.

Now grief, ennui, dissatisfaction, thwarted love laser out of TV screens, the smog-choked air, the heart of every Angeleno still alive.

Tears leak from all the Martians' eyes. Their blue lip-stalks begin to shake. Their putty cheeks puff in and out as they emit fluty wails and wheezing cries.

"Make us beautiful, please," the Martians moan as their jellyfish-brains float to the ceiling of my condo where they pop, like all *my* prayers: unheard, except by me.

He can still fly, and squeeze coal into diamonds, and see through walls and women's clothes; but sometimes, speeding through clouds, he loses control and tumbles like a spent bullet end over end, or forgets where he's going and has to take a taxi home.

He lives alone—Clark Kent, retired reporter—but believes spies sneak into his room and steal his shoes.

Old *Daily Planets* heap up in his hall.

The Health Department calls about cockroaches. He shoves the inspector through a wall.

When Jimmy Olsen dies, then Perry White, he wants to die too. But Earth lacks kryptonite.

Three knives shatter on his wrists. Eight bullets of ascending caliber ping off his skull.

He jumps in front of a train. It derails, killing fifty; he walks away.

His tantrums topple tall buildings. The SWAT Team sent for him retreats with casualties.

The CIA finds Lois in a nursing home. Kidneys shot and colon gone, she says she'll help.

A helicopter lowers her wheelchair into the rubble where Superman sleeps.

She leans down to stroke his cheek. "Superman? It's me."

He jerks upright, eyes baffled. "Who are you?"

"I'm your mother, Superman," she lies.

His brow softens. "I missed you, Mom."

"Do you remember Lois Lane?" she asks.

He scrunches up his face—still young and handsome as a boy's. "Kinda," he says. "She was pretty."

"Lex Luthor has her. Up there." Lois points at Cassiopeia, glittering. "Can you see her?"

Superman squints. "I don't know . . ."

She takes his hand, still strong as steel. "Lois needs you, Superman. You've got to save her."

"Lois," he whispers, and stands.

She straightens his cape.

"Who are you?" he asks.

"Your mother, Superman. Save Lois. Please."

"Save Louis," he says. Stretching hands above his head, he bends his knees.

"Fly, Clark," she says, then grips his cape, and lets his leap yank her up out of her wheelchair.

Her heart slows; then, as the air thins, it stops, her hands relax, and she falls like the last booster of a rocket that, an instant later, begins tumbling end over end toward its home in the stars.

THE POETS

for Ron, Suzanne, and Laurel Ann

"We're closed!" the owner barks as we stroll into the local Steak 'n Ale.

He looks more closely. "Wait! Aren't you . . . ?"

We nod. "The poets."

He scrambles from behind the bar, snags as many of our arms as he can hold, and pulls us in. "Excuse my rudeness . . . such honor . . . I never dreamed . . ."

Tables are cleared, chairs re-arranged, the Closed sign hung so that we won't be disturbed.

"Let me send out for some Dom Perignon," the owner begs. "Anything you'd like, just ask."

"Surprise us," we say with gracious smiles.

"Was the reading sold out like we heard?" a waiter asks as another waiter and two blushing waitresses look on.

"Almost," I say. "Ten thousand paid, give or take."

"There should've been publicity!" The owner stomps his foot in frustration. "And why book you the same night Elvis returned from the grave?!"

Here comes the food: thick prime rib, hearty dark beer, macrobiotics for the health nut, apple juice for the teetotaler.

"Call the kids," the owner whispers to his wife. "Tell them the poets are here."

The girls—Candy and Christine—are beautiful; the boys, Hugh and Sven, are too. "Don't pester the poets, let them eat," their parents scold.

We assure them we don't mind.

Christine in her push-up bra sits in my lap while her siblings entertain my friends. She feeds me morsels from her lips. Finished, she sucks my fingers clean.

"You'll spend the night, won't you?" the owner pleads.

"If you insist . . ."

"Dinner's on the house, of course."

"That's very kind."

Christine leads me to her little pink bedroom. As I help her out of her panty-hose, she muses, "A poet! Mega-cool. Nobody'll believe this in a billion years."

Gods made magic and gave a man, to aid his hay-eaters, a word-consuming thing. "Plant corn," he would say, add the feed-words "I love you," and the thing would suck the sounds in, smile, and carry corn seeds to the field. If he said "I thirst," plus the feed words, the thing would march right off to fetch water.

Directed properly, the thing cleaned house, chopped firewood, and cooked delicious meals. It was warm to sleep beside, and—given the feed words—offered joys of which the man had never dreamed. In a year's time, it even made a miniature of him, attending to its many needs, while the man bragged to his friends.

Only the feed words troubled him. They gave no command, conveyed no data, yet produced results. At first, he had only to say them and the thing would drape itself on him and, even at midday, lead him to bed and open up its mysteries.

Much later, though the feed-words still got results, the thing would stare at him on hearing them, tugging the long hair that screened the twin hills on its chest. "I love you too," it would sigh in its soft voice, then walk away to stare at a wildflower, sunset, bird, or other useless thing, and make vanishing jewels which it called "tears."

When Sheryl Hines, with whom Jesse had traded discs, kissed Don Sanders behind Black Junior High School's auto shop, Jesse said she was a slut, though he feared he wasn't man enough for her, and cried himself to sleep, and cleaned his .22 to kill "Donnie," and called himself *Big Pussy* when he lacked the guts, and only recovered when, over summer break, Sheryl moved away.

If only he had known that babies combine their parents' immune systems (the broader the child's immunities, the better its chance to survive), and that women assess men's immune systems by smelling secretions from the men's apocrine glands, and prefer the scent of men whose immune systems are most different from their own; so Sheryl betrayed him because he smelled more like her father than Don did!

When, junior year, Anne missed her period, and screamed, "I won't get an abortion," Jesse stopped eating, and made plans to flee the country and/or kill himself. When Anne miscarried, he thought it was because God or Satan (he tried both) had heard his prayers.

He might have felt more confident—and spared himself the ego-crushing collapse with that redhead at Garner State Park—if he'd known that he smelled like Anne's brother Ted, and miscarriage is common when couples with similar immune systems conceive.

When Julie had her first orgasm, courtesy of him, Jesse thought it was because he was a sexy guitar-hero whom she loved. He felt so good, he gave the same gift to a dozen other girls, and played great solos, and got hired by Saturnalia, the top band in Dallas, and moved there, leaving Julie behind.

He would have felt less cocky if he'd understood that Julie came because he had a more symmetrical face than her previous boyfriends, all of whom she liked better than him, but since symmetry correlates with health and strength, and since the female orgasm sucks sperm into the uterus, Julie's body was trying to choose the strongest, healthiest male to sire a child.

When Erin dumped her fiancé, Dave, and she and Jesse rutted non-stop for three months, he thought it was because they were soul mates, bathed in the Love that Conquers All.

When her father's nagging drove her back to Dave, Jesse said it was because she was weak, fickle, and loved her father incestuously. He thought it was because he was fatally flawed.

Would he have soaked his liver less in the next year if he had known that, when Erin went on the pill "so we can do it any time," her body thought it was pregnant, and pregnant women prefer the scent of blood relatives, and Dave smelled as well as acted like her dad?

On tour with his band, Numbnuts, Jesse met Jill, a married woman who wanted "a musical child." Since Jill's husband was away on business for just one night, Jesse assumed his sperm would get lost in the crush.

Nine months later, Jill sent Jesse's booking agency a picture of a baby boy who looked like him. (Fathers are more likely to nurture babies that resemble them.)

Jesse spent months sweating a paternity suit, and feeling bad for Jill's husband, whom she called "a wonderful, tone-deaf guy." Jesse would never have cuckolded him if he'd realized Jill's uterus would become a war zone, Jesse's sperm against the husband's, their oval-headed "kamikaze-sperm" butting each other, releasing deadly *acrosome*, while the husband's "blocker-sperm" with their coiled heads formed a cervical barricade to stop Jesse's "egg-getters" from getting through; but because Jesse smelled less like her family than her husband did, and was more symmetrical, she came three times, and sucked Jesse's egg-getters straight into her womb. So, although next night her husband spewed huge numbers of sperm (since men ejaculate more after separation from their partners, trying to overwhelm potential cuckolders), it was too late.

When Jesse's first wife and he failed to conceive, he thought it was because her abortion at sixteen had made her sterile, or pollutants had lowered his sperm count, or she was secretly using contraceptives, since their marriage had gone bad.

Would they have worked harder to reconcile, or saved themselves grief, and divorced sooner, if they'd known that cigar-headed "family-planner sperm," which kill egg-getters, increase in number when a male is stressed the way Jesse was, so that his semen, coupled with his wife's refusal to give him the satisfaction of making her come, had already reached the decision it would take their brains two more years of marital torment to achieve?

Since then, Jesse has remarried, having won his new wife from a boyfriend whose left ear is bigger than his right (though he hides it with long hair), and who wears size 10 on his left foot, 9 on his right.

Jesse's wife and he are intellectually and physically compatible, deeply in love, and committed to monogamy. She's multiply orgasmic with him, and loves his smell, but she was taking birth control pills when they met, and now her doctor says "Go off them for a year."

Will their marriage survive?

The Chairman of a university physics department develops "quite a thing" for pomades.

He doesn't mention it to anyone. Not even in bed to his pretty blonde wife twelve years his junior. Not even in his backyard, playing badminton with his good-looking kids, a girl and a boy, ten and twelve years old respectively, who do well in school, have lots of nice friends, and are perfectly adjusted.

He denies the "thing" to himself. He denies even the need to deny having denied it. He in no way ever, not for one split second, indicates the presence of the "thing." It's just as if the "thing" doesn't exist.

Except it does.

In the lecture hall. In the laboratory. At the beach playing frisbee. At the symphony hearing Beethoven dismembered. At the laundromat washing his hunting pants and his wife's panties the day the washer breaks. At the podium chairing the biggest convocation of world-class physicists in history. Relaxing in his chaise lounge on his fresh-cut lawn warm summer evenings, watching pretty girls bounce by in tans and shorts and halter tops—loving his wife, and reflecting that life has been good to him.

Pomades.

Oh sweet Jesus, pomades.

His Five Proofs of God still flame: memorials to the world-class thinking
a good monk could do on long nights with no electric lights or women,
no gymnastics, or TV to watch them on.

True, when he stated his Argument from Motion, *Since nothing can
move itself, there must have been a First Mover,* he didn't reckon with my
glasses (left on the bathroom counter; found under the bed), or the
famous Disappearing Single Sock.

His Argument from Efficient Causes, loved by lawyers who sue every-
one and thing in the known and unknown world on the grounds that
Client's slip-and-fall *could not have caused itself,* is refuted every time my
mood shifts from calm contentment to seething gray funk with no cause
at all.

His Argument from Possible and Necessary Existence—roughly,
Nothing can come from nothing—has a Shakespearean ring, but is dis-
proved by last night's materializing of a wolf spider on my bathroom
wall.

His Argument from Degrees of Excellence—*Degrees of perfection exist,
so absolute perfection must too*—begs the question "What is perfect?" and
collapses before my first eighteen years, which proved that there did not
exist a boy's room, in this world or out, clean enough to please my mom.

His Argument from Design—*Plants need water, and rain falls; the penis
(mostly) fits the vagina; therefore, God engineered it all*—evaporates, faced
with my weak eyesight and trick knee.

The whole colosseum of Thomist thought crumbles when we grasp
evolution, and how probability can work, given time—when we realize
that Cause & Effect, Being & Non-Being, Beginning & End are human
constructs, and the universe may be uncaused and eternal, or random
and intermittent. If we choose to call it, or what "made" it *God,* okay; but
it won't get us a pony for Christmas, or off a cross.

Assume that Something—God or Googol—did create heaven and
earth. If It doesn't affect my life—if "right" behavior doesn't please It,
and prayers to It do no good—then, as much as I want to believe in It, as
much as ethics and attitudes improve, in general, when people believe—
for my purposes, *It isn't there.*

Still, refuting St. Thom with modern physics is like using a laser to
outshoot a bow.

Faith today is refusing to believe that, if the winner of the marathon wanted to go twenty-six-miles-plus, he should have hired a cab.

Greatness is refusing to think that, since the winner of the mile run ends up right where he began, we might as well kick off our track shoes, swig a cold one, and just chill.

Charity was bored. She hated spending every day with her dull sisters, dressed for church. Her wrists ached from making prayer's two-handed spade. Two-thousand-year-old virgins were absurd!

When Roy Rogers and Dale Evans sang about her at the end of every bloodless, shot-his-gun-right-out-of-his-hand, tediously tame Wild West show, Charity seethed. Oh to kick that damned TV!

Nobody smart believed in virtue anymore. Faith used rouge to keep her face glowing. Hope constantly grumbled, "With my luck . . ."

When the Beach Boys' "Help Me Rhonda" hit number one, "It's like," Charity said, "they're singing to *me*."

While her sisters slept, "Rhonda" went out, conked a hooker with her halo, and swapped clothes.

She started working strip bars, making big bucks as an ex-nun hot to lose her innocence. When her face grew too hard for that, she walked the streets.

She picked up a drug habit. Then another. She took anything she could force up her nose, down her throat, into a vein. "Ears are a waste," she said. "Two good holes with nothing to put in them."

Church-goers felt the change, but thought it was the Mass in English, guitars instead of organs, rap sessions instead of prayers. It seemed easier, now, to kick off Sunday clothes and tell the poor, "Go get a job. Abort babies you can't afford. Smell better. Stop bothering me."

These days, Rhonda purse-snatches and turns five-dollar tricks to feed the monkeys on her back. When all else fails, she hitchhikes to the Red Cross and gives blood. To hell with Hepatitis C and HIV! She gives, and gives, and gives.

The moment I conceive of them, they start to bully me.

"Don't use the f-word," my son pipes with an angry rattle-shake. "I'll say it in front of Gavin's parents when I'm 3, and they won't let me play with him."

"Don't throw a tantrum when the time-share outfit doesn't offer lunch—even if they promised one," my daughter scolds, clutching her Barbie. "Consider, too, the morality of visiting a time-share every time you're in Hawaii—lying to the salesman just to get a *gift*.

"Also, go back to church," she says. "So what if you find the transubstantiation ludicrous, the resurrection wishful thinking, the minister a droning popinjay? Children need God in heaven to feel safe on earth."

"Shave your goatee," sneers my son. "Grow your hair a normal length, even if it's gray and thin. Beards and shaved heads frighten kids. What kind of Dad goes to PTA looking like a Hells Angel, or some superannuated punk?"

"Sell your truck," they chant, "and get an SUV. Stop blowing money on fly-fishing gear. We need piano lessons and new tennis shoes."

"Those *nervous feet* you joke about, and the way you fret and gripe before vacations—control that stuff, or go on Prozac before you turn us into worry-warts like you," my daughter says. "Rethink how you spew dire predictions just to ease your own anxiety; you'll give us nightmares.

"As for your opinions—'Princess Di was a damned leech,' 'Contempt of court's the only sane response'—keep them to yourself. Our innocence will lose us soon enough."

"Learn to cook," my son chimes in. "At least spaghetti and stir-fry! Take a class on patching stucco and fixing drips. Your *Impractical Artist* has lost its charm."

"Pick up your clothes," they chorus. "Wash the dishes, sweep and vacuum, water the ice-plant, prune the roses, learn to tie a Double Windsor. For the first time in your adult life, act your age—which isn't young, let me tell you.

"Drop the term *piece of shit*. And stop laughing at potty humor. '*A Pile in the Woods* by Squatt and Leavitt' is for us to say, and you to send us to our rooms for saying, so we don't grow up disrespecting everything."

"This isn't fair! You spoil my fun," I scream, drop on the floor, and kick.

They fold their little arms and scowl. "Go to your room, old man," they say. "Don't come out till you're a gentleman."

ESCAPE

This tedious room I'm in—ancient tan TV, funereal dresser with chipped mirror, lumpy bed, pretentious poster of a French bread advertisement, wind squeaking through the window like an arseniced rat.

Why have I stayed so long? If I find out someone was using psychology, witchcraft, or any other means to coop me here . . . I could devote my life to hunting such a person, tracking him through jungles, over mountains, across snowy wastes year after year, grinding him down, letting him feel my hot breath on his neck, then drawing back like a skilled lover, prolonging my pleasure until I can stand no more, and leap out of the shadows one dark night and MAKE HIM PAY!

Nothing can keep me here! I'm breaking out. Walking down a long hall (scary, but exciting).

Here's a door. I'll kick it down, damning the consequences.

Oh. It's open.

I'm walking through, enraptured by the Golden Age TV, majestic dresser, mirror scalloped asymmetrically, bed dotted with acupressure points, exquisite still-life of French bread, wind roaring through the window like a victorious God.

A married woman decides she wants an affair—a torrid and abandoned one with masochistic overtones, like in the movies and *Police Gazette*. But she doesn't want to lose control; that would be scary. And she doesn't want to actually have sex. It would be messy and squishy and, well, just *yuck*. It's bad enough with her husband.

She certainly doesn't want her face slapped, or to be spread-eagled in bed, or hung by her arms and whipped by some deranged he-man Nazi-war-criminal type. She bruises easily; and pain—well, it hurts.

She certainly doesn't want to be subservient. Hasn't she raised two kids (and lost her figure doing it), and cleaned house for an ungrateful bastard every day for years? And aren't women making more strides by the minute, pioneering new frontiers? If some macho bullshitter thinks he can cow her, he needs another think, and soon!

The very idea makes her so depressed she eats a dozen Oreos, takes a valium, crawls into bed and masturbates, then falls asleep and dreams that, dressed in a black chain-mail bikini, she's struggling up the face of a rock-slide that blocks the entry to a Golden Tower from which hairy barbarians with gory scimitars and rapine in their eyes are simultaneously leaping and not leaping down around her, uttering blood-curdling, blood-uncurdling cries.

SOMETHING NOT STUPID

I've been having small thoughts lately: bread crumbs instead of last year's layer cakes.

I used to think about love, war, injustice, sunsets, the existence of God—things people care about. It sounds stupid to mention what I thought about, though my thoughts were much praised.

Now my best thoughts are "a pair of slippers"; "freckle"; "place touched by a unicycle."

First I wanted to make sense. Then I wanted not to make sense. Now I want only to say something not stupid.

My dirty socks smell like hyacinths which smell like dirty socks.

I stride toward the ticket booth, my last ten-dollar-bill trembling like a reluctant bride's hand in my grip. I don't want to give it away . . .

But wait—who's that cashier? Can it be me?

"Man, am I glad to see *you!*" I say. My ten-spot jumps back to my wallet's warm embrace. "I'll just go in . . ."

"Ten dollars, please."

Halfway through the turnstile, I stop. "Hold on. You're talking to yourself."

"All the more reason you pay. If a man can't trust himself, who *can* he trust?"

"The issue isn't trust; it's self-interest," I say. "Shut your eyes. I'll walk in, and no one's the wiser."

He shakes his head. "I'll bet you cheat at solitaire."

"Whose fault is that?! You like to win as much as I do."

Those green eyes I thought I knew so well grow stern. "People are waiting. Pay me, or step out of line."

"You must be kidding! If you won't do yourself a favor, who will?"

"It's no favor to reward dishonesty."

"Come off it, Ace! You sound like Mom and Dad."

"Why act surprised? You've read Freud on the Superego."

Only the glass window keeps me from smashing his smug face.

"To hell with you," I snarl, and stalk away, and don't realize, until I'm soaked with sweat, and everyone I see has goat-horns and a tail, just how deep the trouble is I'm in.

pretended to be a foot bridge across a drainage ditch.

"Pay the bridge a penny," said a little handwritten card by a coffee cup full of pennies. So travelers would drop a penny in the cup if they were honest, ignore the card if they were cheap, or steal from the cup if they were scum. But whatever they were, when they reached the middle of the bridge, it reared up and thrust a large, professionally lettered sign in their faces: "GIVE ME EVERYTHING YOU'VE GOT, OR I TOSS YOU IN THE CHASM."

Naked people could always be seen hurrying off the bridge, which brought more people hurrying on to stare at private parts for free.

Soon the bridge became so rich, it hired a younger bridge to cheat people while it toured the world, spanning grand and scenic vistas, letting the little fools swarm on it, full of love.

Jeremy Porcino, M.D., decides that what fat people need is a good thumping, that's all.

He thumps his wife's fat sausage-arm when she gets out of bed.

"You don't love me," she whines, and eats a ham, three waffles loaded with whipped cream and marmalade, six raspberry Danish, and a dozen devilled eggs for breakfast.

He thumps her multi-rolled, bread-pudding gut that bounces and jiggles even when she's sitting still.

"You don't love me," she cries, and eats a whole turkey, a large anchovy pizza, a box of smoked eels, a sliced veal tongue sandwich, a plate of puff-pastry filled with little clams and sea urchin butter, a filet of sea bass in a crunchy black coat of peppercorns, set on a bed of leeks cooked into an almost-jam and lightly splashed with vinegar, a quart of chocolate ice cream, and a one pound box of Almond Roca for lunch.

He thumps her vast, wobbly buttocks that hang over the largest dinner chair like mashed potato mountains sliding to the floor.

"You don't love me," she wails, and eats five orders of sizzlin' shrimp fajitas, a dozen deep-fried, cheese-filled rice balls, a plate of sautéed sweetbreads with stuffed zucchini blossoms and just a touch of truffle, a pair of round baked potatoes, partly diced, mixed with *creme fraiche* and caviar, spooned back into the skins and served on crusted thrones of salt, plus a lemon meringue pie, fifty oatmeal cookies, and a side of beef for dinner.

He thumps her gigantic, puckery thighs—like twin elephant seals, lashed tight by pubic hair, dragging their puffed, blubbery bodies across the living room.

"You don't love me," she weeps, and eats three ducks, four whole blackened redfish, a plate of oysters, crab, and scallops in sour cream, a mushroom pie in a delectable Moroccan pastry, oysters in Thai green curry, rabbit with figs roasted with thyme and bacon, and a whole cheese-cake served with a leg of lamb, prunes, and Armagnac ice cream for an after-dinner snack.

"All right, you win. I love you," Doctor P says as they're going to bed.

"Good," she says. "Bring me a braised duck with tiny baked turnips and straw potatoes, a bucket of fish soup, and *brioche* with warm apple-sauce to help me sleep, please won't you Dear? I'm starved."

AT SUPPER TIME

—*for Russell Edson*

A roast becomes resentful and spins, spilling juice in Father's lap just as he's about to carve.

"You treat me like a piece of meat," the roast whines.

"You *are* a piece of meat," Father explains.

"I wish you'd treat *me* like a piece of meat. Or *anything* besides your maid," grumbles Mother.

"You don't listen. I don't know why I bother talking!" the roast yells.

"You never *have* talked before," Father reminds. "I like that better. Talking food upsets my stomach. And disturbs the potato chilluns."

"There you go again with racial slurs," Mother complains.

"Are you calling those four earth-turds here our brothers?" the couple's human children shrill.

The potatoes jump out of their dish and wobble toward the table's edge.

"The Earth, their mother, is our mother too. We're all brothers," Father reminds.

"That's it. Give Earth the credit, and gloss over me," Mother sighs.

"These by-products of Earth's digestion are a threat to our inheritance," the human children shriek.

"Your inheritance consists of this roast meat," Father explains.

"What?! My dowry squandered?! I want lawyers!" Mother screams.

"See?! See?! I'm a possession!" the roast shouts, sloshing around on its platter like a log rolled by the fly walking on it.

"Your dowry was these potatoes, which you forced me to adopt," Father reminds Mother.

"They're my brothers. What else could I do?" Mother screams.

"Kill the pretenders!" the human children shriek. They pick up knives and forks, and stab the potatoes.

White potato innards fly around the room.

"Help! Fratricide!" Mother screams.

"Police! Police! I want to report some murders," Father explains into the telephone. "My sons and heirs. Yes. I'm just sick."

"I'm getting cold!" the roast howls, slicing itself and flopping plate to plate. "I'm drying out! Come on, cowards! Indulge your depraved appetites on me!"

45

He finds himself in a country of worms disguised as kings. Him, a real king, disguised as a worm! How he aches to find a throne and take command. But before he can tear off his costume and make decrees, the population is upon him, screaming,"Look! Bait for the royal trout!"

A huge hand grabs him. He squirms free, drops for what seems miles, and dives into the ground with shovels hacking at his heels.

He plunges deeper as the yelling, blare of trumpets, clank and scrape of digging, fade like footsteps winding up a tower.

Memory fades with them. Castles. Falcons. Chests brimming with gold. Armies at his command. Lithe wenches. Groveling princes . . .

His thoughts bleach white as grass under a fallen tree. Gradually he accepts the core of dirt that worms through his bowels as he digs. Slowly he recalls the taste, smell, peristaltic rhythm of the earth.

The manager of a franchised fast-food restaurant is convinced that a dry well just outside of town conceals his "Secret Name." This name, he read in a pamphlet which he found shoved under his windshield wiper, *encapsulates* his *True Identity,* and therefore functions as *a personal soda straw into the Cosmic Fuel Supply.* So even though he's proud of his parent company and believes that it, and he, make *a major contribution,* he quits his job, buys mining gear, and drives to the well.

There he finds a wooden bucket and an odd pattern of rocks which he suspects to mean *Secret Name Buried Here.* He lowers himself down the well—interesting for its age and the bones strewn on the bottom, but which reveals no Secret Name.

He starts to dig

He digs for longer than he would have thought possible, nibbling on dried apricots and beef jerky from the local backpacking store. After a while, he forgets to eat, forgets to sleep, forgets to do anything but dig.

Hours pass. Or is it days? Or is it years? The temperature turns colder and colder, then hotter and hotter, then colder and colder until he pulls himself out on a frozen mountainside.

A monastery gleams in the snowy distance, so he staggers toward it, trying not to step on his white beard. He barely manages to drag himself inside before collapsing by a stone pillar on which strange letters writhe.

"That's got to be my Secret Name! What does it mean?" he croaks as Death pulls its gunny sack over his knees.

The monks jabber in Tibetan.

The gunny sack shinnies up his torso as an old American woman totters out of a corner and starts to tell her life story, which involves a professorship in Eastern Thought, a brief fling with a *yeti,* and a succession of heartbreaks.

The gunny sack is up to the man's neck. He struggles now. He won't be bagged like steer manure!

"What's that writing say?" he snaps at the old woman. "I haven't got all day!"

She clears her throat. Just as Death brains him and hauls his sack away, she tells him, "Worm."

It starts as a list in *The Therapist* of licensees who have lost theirs.

After a year, to add "pizzazz," a new designer draws a black spider at the top of the page. Six months later, the offense goes in: drug abuse; insurance fraud; sex with clients; gross negligence . . .

Fearing display in these journalistic stocks, therapists abandon Rolfing, rebirthing, primal screams. They keep good records, give up hugging patients, smoking, drinking, and having affairs.

Instead of reinforcing sexy talk, they hold their ears. "Don't tell me," they plead. "I don't want to know."

The Spider Page grows more detailed:

"Respondent drove to a home in south central Los Angeles, was offered a Bud Lite, drank it, then bought two ounces of cocaine for $2,000: an exceptional deal."

"Dressed as a mailman, Respondent knocked on Patient's door. 'Special Delivery,' he called.

"The patient—never good with metaphor—answered the door wearing a towel. 'My bathtub's plugged,' she said. 'Can you fix it, please?'"

What kind of drone would read "Self-Defeating Personality Disorder: A Profile," or "A Day in the Life of a Managed Care Provider," when she can flip right to the Spider "Page": now more than half the magazine?

Finding that Listees can rack up fat speaking fees, some clinicians fabricate misdeeds. They hire editors and ghost-writers, bypass the licensing board, and send "confessions" straight to *The Therapist*.

"It was a bright day in October, mockingbirds trilling, his wife clinking her coffee cup in the kitchen: a perfect day to call in sick, drive to the mountains, and enjoy some therapeutic fall trout fishing. But Dr. Forrest Gelding of Santa Barbara, CA, license number *****, couldn't stop thinking of Dalila, the busty fourteen-year-old histrionic with bulimia whose case he'd been assigned . . ."

Subscribers to *The Therapist* now greet their mail as eagerly as British crowds once greeted news of Little Nell. Magazine in hand, they lock their office doors, unplug their phones, and sink into their leather chairs to read, or work for blissful hours on their own stories, deaf to the coyote chorus of unanswered psychic cries.

This morning when I check my e-mail after my computer has been down for weeks because our wisecracking Macintosh expert (about my age) dropped dead of a heart attack, and no one else in the Office of Technical Services could fix it (my computer) until now— when I scroll down my unread messages looking for prizes I've won, or love-notes from sinuous strangers, all I need is to see a message from my Union President titled, ALERT!

I know Internet is to Hoax as Rat to Plague; still, I open ALERT! first, and read, not how Management continues plotting to dissolve the Union and enslave the Workers, but how three Chicago women were hospitalized with fever, chills, and vomiting, followed (quickly) by paralysis and death—how there were no signs of trauma, but autopsies revealed blood toxicity—how these three women, strangers to each other, had all visited Big Chappie's restaurant at Blare Airport within days of their demise—how the Health Department closed the restaurant, inspecting food, water, and air conditioning, to no avail.

I'd have much preferred, on such a wind-kissed morning, to read about *Das Apfelessig*, the German elixir that dissolves fat, allowing happy weiner-munchers "to blitz away three pounds a day, fourteen pounds in a week." But no, I have to read how, soon after the three deaths, a waitress at Big Chappie's was rushed (always rushed, never driven leisurely) to the hospital. She'd been on vacation (snorkeling, luaus, sex on the beach), and only went to Chappie's for her pay. She didn't eat or drink, but did use the restroom.

A toxicologist, acting on the kind of hunch that pays off on TV but rarely in life, went to the restaurant (closed and shuttered), lifted the women's toilet seat, and found, clinging to the wood, a small pink spider.

It's 6 a.m. Outside my office, the world is a black-and-white photo, underexposed but of astonishing detail: the high-rise next door, and every car in the parking lot outlined as if by charcoal. Leaves shimmer on their trees like schools of small, dark fish.

This would be the perfect time for me to learn how vinegar's acetic acid breaks down fat—how, since no one can drink a quart of vinegar per day, German scientists at Benz Laboratories (like the car?) combine the sweet pectins in apple cider with concentrated acetic acid to make their miracle. But no, I have to learn that the pink stowaway proved to be the deadly South American blush spider, *Arachnius gluteus*, which thrives in damp, dark places—i.e., under toilet seats.

I'd have quivered with excitement to learn that, taken three times daily, *Das Apfelessig* unlocks fat cells, forcing fat to drain away. To think that my excess weight, including the spare tire I can't lose no matter what, could be "flushed out like water gushing from a tap!" Not only that—taking these pills would let me gorge, and still lose weight! Food is comfort, and comfort matters in these anxious days.

Hans Weidermeyer of Berlin states, "I love beer. Love schnitzel. Am crazy for strudel. Maybe that's why for years I've had size forty-six waistline. But with *Das Apfelessig*, I lopped eleven inches off my waist in just thirty-three days, without giving up my favorite foods." That would be something to look forward to: reward for bothering to climb into my imported Hunkajunk with its cocked bumper, dinged fenders and slipping clutch, then drive thirty miles in viscous traffic to a cluttered cubicle with a computer barely kept chugging by weekly repairs, and which drops off-line once a month at least—proof how little my company needs me.

But no, I have to learn that a lawyer from L.A. collapsed (always collapsed, never lay down carefully) the day after he changed planes at Blare Airport, but did *not* go to Big Chappie's. His autopsy showed a puncture wound on his right buttock. *And* his flight originated in Brazil.

The Civilian Aeronautics Board inspected the toilets on all South American flights, found blush spiders on four of the planes, and concluded that the spiders have invaded the U.S., and the public is "at risk."

Peachy. My dad died of a stroke, my cholesterol is genetically high, my wife's family has a history of breast cancer, every week there's a scare concerning some incurable African bleeding brain death, or mutating TB bacillus boiling out of Russian jails, or terrorist Armageddon, and— forget my wife and me—we've got a one-year-old, at risk for everything.

I love that *Das Apfelessig* requires no prescription or FDA approval. I've dropped the ball a time or two, but I'm Golden Glove compared to most doctors, and all governmental agencies.

I love that the pills are *natural*. Maybe the world is human-friendly after all! Spider venom dissolves flesh. And fat is flesh. Why can't it be dissolved easily, simply, healthfully?

And why not other things? Mistakes. Sadness. Time.

So many people I'd love to see again. Love to fish with. Love to help make Christmas cookies. Love to let them teach me the full nelson. Am crazy to unhook their bra, and feel the weight of their breasts one more time.

Sure, *Das Apfelessig* could be a scam, like thigh-wraps and fat-dissolving creme.

"Benz Laboratories"? Come on.

And that talk of strudel, combined with the American "lopped off"? Give me a break.

Big Chappie's sounds fake too. Big Chaps-My-Ass. Speaking of which, *Arachnius gluteus?* I don't think so.

Blare airport is probably a take-off on Blair or Blaire. I'm pretty sure it's *Civil*, not *Civilian* Aeronautics Board, and Journal of the *American*, not United, Medical Association.

I'll look these things up when I find time. For now, I flinch when I sit on the pot.

What kind of world have I brought my son into, where con-men feed off the fat, who only want love like everyone else, and not to get diabetes, have their knees go out, and die before they're forty—where people spread terror just to add a pinch of cayenne to the thin gruel of their lives—where, if there are no blush spiders, there sure *could* be.

No wonder workers put so much faith in their Union. No wonder I find, at the bottom of the *Das Apfelessig* ad, scratched in an unknown hand, beside a happy-face, "In Vinegar We Trust."

A KING

A king is too fat, so he declares himself thin. His subjects, who are thin, he declares fat, so that no foreigner will say, "The king is *thin,* and his subjects are *thin;* but the king is not like his subjects. Someone's lying."

But since a king should not be *too* thin, or people will think him poor and lose respect, the king eats more than ever—eats until he looks like a maggot in a king suit, and declares himself "just right."

And because a king's subjects should not be fat, or they'll seem lazy, the subjects must diet. Which they do until they're skeletons.

The king is furious. All these bare bones stink of treason. He declares his subjects "traitors," and proclaims his "royal joy" that they are dead.

By midday, though, the king is hungry, with no one to bring him food. He hems and haws, and finally pardons everyone.

"You are alive," declares the king, anticipating grateful cheers, then the rush to bring his dinner.

"You are alive. *You are alive!* YOU ARE ALIVE!" commands the king.

"Traffic's awful," says my colleague as we ride the elevator to our floor.

"It is," I say. "The only time I've seen it worse was the day my wife's mom died. We were due at the funeral home by noon, but I was having an affair, and couldn't pull myself away from my little sword-swallower. Once I did, I hit the traffic. When I finally made it home, my wife had overdosed on Xanax, and vomited on our Persian rug. Two thousand dollars, and I had to throw it out."

I'm helping a new guy stretch in Tae Kwon Do class, when he gasps, "Jesus, I'm beat!"

"Me too," I say. "I get so tired here, I thought I must have AIDS. My psychiatrist suspected Epstein-Barre, but the tests were negative, so he put me on Elavil. That made me impotent and gave me hemorrhoids, which ruled out anal intercourse, so I stopped the meds, but now I'm suicidal half the time."

"Bastards," the man in line behind me at Circuit City snarls as we watch a newscaster announce, on Big Screen TV, "Congress has cut Welfare again."

"I was on Welfare for years," I say. "It supported my drug habit. When I wasn't smashed, I fathered kids: nine of the little bastards, so to speak. In my spare time, I robbed liquor stores. Now that Swami's turned my life around, I think all Welfare leeches should be shot, or banished at the very least."

This from me, a lifetime liberal Democrat!

"Fuck the homeless," I say. "Fuck their ratty clothes and long faces and sloppy, misspelled signs. We all paid taxes to educate those bums. They should've learned!"

Am I a silence-phobe? Do I dread more than death the stifled yawn as someone thinks, "Six billion people, and I'm stuck next to him"?

Do I fear that my partner feels burdened by the need to speak, and so I lift the conversation off his back? Do I feel so unworthy that only by cracking my bones and offering my juiciest marrow will I be suffered to stay?

Am I so guilt-wracked I'll seize any chance to confess anything? Is this my Jungian shadow, that—as opposed to murder, which hides very well—will out? Is the Imp of the Verbose not a metaphor, but a flesh-and-blood homunculus that moves my jaw, larynx, and tongue? Do we create the world through metaphors, and experience that in which we believe?

My cousin believes her boyfriend will marry her. On the other hand, he tells me she's so neurotic and they fight so much, he has to smoke a bowl of "skunk" just to e-mail her.

She subscribes to *Modern Bride,* is choosing china, and hums Mendelssohn's wedding march all day.

When I see her next, what will I say?

Then there is the question: how to disrobe for swimming?

If a girl simply strips naked, she's immodest. If she takes off some clothes but leaves others on, she's still undressing, her motions sure to spawn lewd thoughts—the way seeing a mother strolling with her child suggests nights of abandoned passion.

Is it better to arrive predressed in a swimsuit, or to swim dressed in "street" clothes? Doesn't the one show too much skin, and the other show the strong desire *not* to show skin, which conjures visions of the most intimate skin?

And doesn't the failure to swim on a warm, sunny day suggest a wish to hide? And doesn't that imply feelings of guilt and shame, which bring to mind those body parts with which guilt and shame are linked?

There can be but one solution: to undress without undressing, swim without swimming, in the manner of one who, hearing sparrows chirp in the cherry tree outside his window, watches and enjoys them, at the same time not hearing, watching, or enjoying them at all.

He was furiously straightening the room when I arrived. While I waited to be offered a drink, he straightened it twice more.

"Why?" I asked, and poured myself a Zombie made with seven different kinds (I pretended) of tap water, since tap water was all he had.

"It's my wife," he confessed. "The three hours a week she's home, she does nothing but primp for her next week out, and complain that nothing *neat* happens here. I thought a small pun might lighten her load— indicate concern, the willingness to go to lengths. You know?"

I indicated, or I hope I did, that I knew more than I was telling. I swigged my Zombie like an oracular spring, then leapt (I had been sitting) to my feet.

"Plays on words won't win her back! She suffers from acute Deficiency of Marvels. Give her MARVELS! Be her doorway to the miraculous. Her ladder out of the mundane. Bring her home a sasquatch or a Loch Ness monster. Capture a UFO. Master some occult science . . ."

"Marbles! That's it! I'll buy her a sack of marbles," he muttered, messing up the room again.

My sequined trunks flash like a thousand cigarette lighters in Madison Square Garden, where I beat the bejeezus out of shadows until my arms and legs and neck are loose. Loose as a goose. A warm goose. Extremely warm, hence my ring name.

I never really liked that name, and like it less when loudspeakers blare the *Space Odyssey* theme, and my opponent, in a silver space suit, bounds into the ring.

What possessed me to choose "Feelings" as my theme?

When my opponent unscrews his helmet, and I recognize Joe Louis in his prime, I think, "Uh-oh." I'm barely a welterweight. My fists feel slow as lorises. Joe's left hook scythes the air.

My corner-men say, "We'll be right back." Then they run.

Alone as a man in a gas chamber, I sit waiting for the bell.

Thank God, a work crew appears. Bustling like ants—in fact, they *are* ants—they dismantle the ring.

The spectators pile into cars and roar away.

My promoter rolls up in a tank. "Hop in, Goose," he says, and drives to a new ring.

This time I enter to the funeral march from Beethoven's Seventh. My punches pop. My flurries blaze. My legs are tireless pogo sticks.

Better yet, my opponent's a toddler. He can't even lift his gloves.

"Lemme at him," I think, fists making shadow-monsters on the wall.

A man dressed in pajamas is arguing a case before a snowman. The lawyer (as he must be) speaks in a loud voice, striking what he hopes is a dramatic pose each time he makes an irrefutable point.

The judge sits in his black robes, melting.

The lawyer calls witnesses. But the one who takes the stand is never the one he called. So he calls a new witness, thinks of what he should have asked the old, and can't relocate him in the packed courtroom.

Now he insists that, with his knowledge of character, he can tell the judge exactly what each witness *would* have said. He gives examples, in the very words, with the very accent!

The judge keeps melting. His robes are soaked. His powdered wig has slipped over his eyes.

The lawyer argues louder. He's just realized that he is the defendant, too.

He pounds his fist on the huge books he keeps bringing "respectfully" to the court's attention. He refers to exhibits "A through double-D"—more and more inconsistent, praying no one notices, praying he can brass it out.

The judge keeps melting.

Only his top-hat is visible above the bench. His corncob pipe, his coal eyes and teeth, have hit the floor. Now, gavel-like, his carrot nose begins to fall.

Overnight, Jim's tortoise. Keith, has changed into an auk.

"How thoughtful," Jim says, once the shock wears off. "Something wants to teach me about change."

By next morning, his TV has changed into a set of cowbells; his electric shaver, a bowl of wax fruit. He still has an electric shaver, but only because his dentures have changed into one. Luckily, his gums have changed into a set of real teeth; so he can chew, although his corns have changed into a trick knee, worsening his limp.

"It's very nice of you, Professor, teaching me to detach from earthly things, which disappear and break your heart," Jim tells whatever's listening.

A cracking and crunching, along with stabbing pains in both his feet, reveal that his New Zealand sheepskin slippers have changed into souvenir ashtrays, now shattering under his weight.

No sooner does he plug in his coffee pot than it changes into a cowboy hat.

"All right, all right, I get the message," grumbles Jim. "By now, I should've earned my Ph.D. in Change."

He sits down in his easy chair to pick glass-slivers from his feet. Too bad the chair has changed into an irate dachshund, which sinks its little fangs into his rear.

"Ow! Goddammit, now you're making fun of me!" yells Jim. "It's bad pedagogy to make fun!"

Before his eyes, his computer changes into an ant farm; his clothes closet, into a box of moldy Christmas pears; his Acura Legend, a tree stump; his house, a Mayan temple overgrown with vines.

"Is this a learning experience, or a cosmic diddling?" Jim wheezes, and finds he's changed into a bent old man.

He wakes to find it fitted on his left calf like a boot.

Is this a hospital, doctors lurking, poised to break bad news? No, it's his bedroom: white cottage cheese ceiling, smoke detector hanging, open-mouthed, stripped of its battery.

He puts his weight on the foot: stiff, but no worse than usual.

The thing seems carved of smooth white pine. A skillful job. It even blends well with his skin.

"I can live with this," he thinks, and goes to work.

That night, he dreams he's leading his fiancée over fields of baking bread. They have to leap from crust to crust or sink into hot dough and be *caramelized*. They've almost made it to safety—a Hawaiian *heiau*—when the crust breaks.

He wakes to find his foot has changed to lead: gray-glinting in dawn light. He doubts that he can lift this false foot; but he does. He puts on three socks to muffle any tendency to clunk, and starts his day.

That night, he shows the foot to his fiancée. "See any difference?"

"You ask that every night," she says. "Not asking would be different."

Next day his foot is the porcelain dentists use on teeth. The day after, the foot is marble; the next, iron.

The foot is always functional, and blends in well. Even at the beach, no one can tell.

After he's married, on nights when he can't sleep, he slips from bed— wife locked in dreams—and tiptoes to the living room. There, wrapped in the welcoming dark, he falls asleep, lulled by the shimmer of his foot, its ghostly gleam.

What would he do? What would become of him, stricken with Zinjanthropus disease?

There were no precedents. Still, he refused to fool himself. The thing was what it was. How else explain the receding forehead, increased stoop, flattening nose, thick body-hair (on him, who'd shunned beaches, cursing his smooth chest)? And this craving to sit in a cave by a sacred fire, and gnaw giant-sloth leg!

How he envied pregnant women, whose pickles-and-yogurt cravings were smiled at, satisfied, encouraged.

Like any smart young man, he'd put off marriage until he'd sown his wild oats, and put off sowing until his job left him time. How would he find a mate now? How would he rise in his firm? The grappling hooks he'd thrown over that vice-presidency—and which had caught!—were turning brittle and brown as winter vines.

Try as he would, he couldn't conceptualize the way he used to.

Find a woman, he mused, stifling an urge to stalk small, juicy, horse-like creatures. *Drag her to my lair in the mountains.*

We will learn which gods rule where, learn how to please them and avoid their wrath. We will sing songs to the moon and sun, eat and wear what the forest gives. We'll watch our old lives bound away like antelope, glad to feel our brains shrink, walls dissolving between us and everything.

An orangutang sits crouched in the back seat of your Hyundai when you open the front door to get in.

He's not real big, and doesn't look fierce—nothing like that *Murders in the Rue Morgue* marauder which slashed a woman's head off, and crammed her up a chimney.

This one looks embarrassed, shy.

He stops scratching when you glare at him. ("Fleas," you think. "Swell.") His hair is red like yours, though shaggier. "Old Man of the Forest," Borneo natives call orangutangs.

Does he remember swinging tree to tree in Borneo?

He looks as if he does.

He must have watched you watching him hide underneath his gunny sack: reluctant star of the Monkey House.

Did he hear you tell the woman next to you, "Gosh, he looks sad"? You spoke to her because, in general, women seem kinder than men. But this one snorted "Creep!" and stalked away.

By whatever means, he's here.

Congratulations. Your soft heart's picked up another leech.

He'll get you fined or thrown in jail. No way can you afford to feed him. Aw, but hey—he can wash dishes, sweep floors, something . . .

Maybe he can be a conversation piece! He can't drag your love life lower, that's for sure.

You wonder who's saving whom as you hiss, "stay down," drive past the parking lot attendant's scowl, and head for home.

Anesthetized by sleep, J.C. gives birth to an idea of a woman. He wakes to find her curled comfortably in his arms.

He kisses her. Perfect response!

He wallows in the feel of her round breasts, smooth thighs, pubic puff. Her warm breath and grateful sighing drive him wild.

He makes love to her: the best he's ever had!

"Drunk with passion! At last," he thinks. Over and over.

The two stay in bed all day. When the phone rings, they giggle and ignore it. They agree on everything.

Across town, in a lovely modern office, the Boss slams down his phone and raves. The phrase *Ax the little bastard* may be worn out for all time.

But when, at 5:00, his secretary appears with a large margarita and no panties, he cools down. Reconsiders.

For the third time this week, he calls his wife to say he's working late, while outside his office and J.C.'s bachelor apartment, the giant hand that had been painting a swirly orange, red, and purple picture of the sky, blacks it out, throws in the moon and a few stars, and glides away.

Some days he only has the regular, cold ones. Still, he loves roaring down oak-canopied streets, his truck clanging "Night on Bald Mountain" as he shrieks "Hot popsicles!" and the kids who've surged out of their houses, waving Mom's limp dollar bills, stampede back inside, wailing.

The days his truck plays "Stars and Stripes Forever," he's a hero, trying to make an All-American buck selling popsicles bought cheap because they melted and re-froze. "Hot popsicles," the trade calls them—texture more granular, shape less perfect than ideal; but what do kids care, if the color's there, the sugar's real?

Not *hot* as in stolen; he wouldn't stoop to that.

Hot as in *spicy*—Szechuan popsicles, Mexican cayenne popsicles. Hot as in *exciting, explosive, desirable*—hot car, hot wire, hot date. But also the metaphysical, theoretical popsicle that keeps its sex-toy shape while steaming hot as any toddy, cappuccino, or spiced wine: something to lick on a January night as flames pogo in the fire-pit, and snow feathers the house.

Ahhh, for a last hot popsicle before bed!—solid and sizzling, delivered through the mind, like those times the lost love-of-your-life comes top-less to your birthday party, and you kiss her breasts in front of everyone. You're all adults; sexual attraction is good.

She tastes like hot cherries, perfect for the popsicles I mean.

He's there when I get home: white beard, Charles Atlas muscles—just like in the Sistine Chapel. I feel like Adam when he offers to shake hands.

"God," I say, "You haven't aged a day . . ."

He wastes no time. "You know that test you bombed in tenth grade? The one that kept you out of Honors Math?"

I nod.

"Misgraded; you deserved an *A*. Remember not making the track team?"

I nod.

"They meant to cut *Chad* Webb. Damn fool coach mixed up the names."

"What about Yale?" I prompt. "Why didn't I get in?"

"Politics." He spits. "One spot was left. You had it. Then the dean's grandson applied."

I shake my head. "I thought I was a total bleb."

"That's over now. I'm here to make things right." He smiles and nudges me. "Remember Jo Ann?"

How could I forget? I agonized for weeks before I asked her out. She looked me up and down, and said, "'Fraid not, Zit-Master."

Suddenly she's here.

"I was wild for you," she whispers, unzipping her dress.

I look around. God has discreetly vanished.

"I was scared of sex," she pants. "You were *so sexy*. All the girls were wild for you."

"Thank God," I wake up sobbing happily. "Thank God."

Nothing pleased him any more. Not browbeating nephew Donald. Not foreclosing on widows. Not even dumping a truckload of double coupons on the Safeway checker, or admiring his house-high ball of string. More and more, his money bin looked like a tomb.

In three years of analysis, he learned that his wealth was overcompensation for "Oedipal issues." He managed to lose some of each, but still felt lousy.

Donald, Daisy, and the boys were sympathetic; but he knew his assets were their main concern.

He tried drugs, EST, Eckankar, Scientology.

He tried threesomes, foursomes, group gropes, B & D, S & M.

He tried astrology, numerology, palmistry, mineral baths, rolfing, nude encounters, channeling. He bought crystals, and stared at them for days.

More and more nothing.

A lumpy, crab-like misery gnawed his heart. But the world's finest specialists swore his health was "perfect."

Finally, after a *Sixty Minutes* exposé, he went to Oregon to see guru Baghwan Pym.

"I've done everything I ever wanted to," he told the Master. "I've chased the Flying Dutchman through the Sargasso Sea, faced Moby Dick and Blackbeard's ghost, seen the pyramids from inside, and talked with Ramses in the mummified flesh. I've been marooned in Bora Bora, hobnobbed with yetis in the Hindu Kush, turned yak butter into gold. I've escaped enough sharks to swallow Miami and Malibu combined, discovered lost Inca cities and Buddhist temples so deep in Southeast Asia that the natives have never smelled napalm. Every time, I've turned a profit. I'm the richest duck in the world. And I feel *bad.*"

The guru said nothing.

The guru's representative said, "Give us your possessions. Baghwan Pym will give you peace."

Scrooge wrote a check, hoping munificence would spark spiritual rebirth. But the more he saw of the faithful and their town, "Pympuram," the less he liked it. Pym looked like just another weirdo with a scam.

After phoning a stop payment on his check, Scrooge started the long walk to his Lear jet.

It was a gray November day, Winter's wind-broom whisking Fall away.

He passed a pond where mallards bobbed for food. "Hey grandpa," quacked a big one with a shimmering green head. "It's almost time."

Amazed, Scrooge realized that he'd understood.

"Come on in," a little brown duck quacked. "Take off those spats and swim."

Scrooge suspected this was what his analyst meant by "psychotic break," but he took off his clothes and waddled in.

The cold water felt good. But his feet were barely wet when, one by one, the ducks began to fly away.

"Where are you going?" he called in English. "Don't you like me?"

"Come on," the little brown duck quacked. "Come on!"

Without his asking them, his wings began to flap. They felt stiff, but lifted him. He felt something break loose inside, and he was quacking, really quacking, not just speaking English through his nose.

He made three loops and a back flip just to prove he could, then started to climb, wings cupping air the way they cupped water that time he dived for the world's biggest black pearl and barely escaped the giant clam, shooting toward the water's surface just the way he's shooting toward the sun right now, clouds like eider down around him, his little pile of clothes shrinking beside the shrinking pond, the streets and cars and houses shrinking into nothing as he climbs higher toward the joyful quacking overhead, and takes his place in the dark arrow that streaks across the wide, opening sky.